Wild Bill

Matthew Caldwell

DEDICATION

This book is dedicated to Drema and Bill Caldwell. Mom, thank you for keeping this great family together and Wild Bill thank you for the memories.

Matthew Caldwell

CONTENTS

INTRODUCTION

Most people have at least one crazy family member. Whether it's the wild uncle who considers it his solemn duty to get drunk at family weddings, or the estranged cousin who is always on the wrong side of the law, most of us can relate to having "black sheep" in our lives. For my family, one with no shortage of interesting personalities, that person is undoubtedly my father— William Norman Caldwell. Affectionately known by friends and complete strangers as "Wild Bill," he is what some would call an "old school" New Yorker: born in Brooklyn, 35 years with the N.Y.P.D., heavy New York accent, and fully believes the world ends at the New York City limits. Yet with all these uniquely defining characteristics, the thing that truly makes my father "Wild Bill," is that he will do anything for his kids. And I mean *anything*.

Before launching into stories about my father, I am obliged to clarify one critical fact. There is nobody in this world like my mother, Drema Caldwell. I could write another book about her and all she has done to keep this family together. The Caldwells have all the drama and conflict of any American family, but I would add with more intensity and fervor. Drema is the one who has always kept us on track. Even when she and Wild Bill separated many years ago, she insisted that we all maintain relationships with our father and she never let anything stand in the way of keeping the family intact. She is truly special. Sorry Pops, you're the best and I could never even dream of having any other father, but nobody even comes close to our mom, the greatest woman to ever grace God's green earth. Besides, without her putting up with you for all these years, none of these stories would have ever even come about!

But this time, she will take a back seat, like she so often does. Why? Because she knows that keeping the story of Wild Bill to herself would be a great injustice to the rest of humanity. Drema has witnessed this man's shenanigans more than anyone else and knows truly in her heart that it's time to let the rest of the world know. Fathers around the world (which I hope to be someday): please begin taking notes now, because this is how it's done.

This book is a collection of eleven stories about the amazing, albeit ridiculous, things my father has done for his family. There are also few shorter stories that I included in between chapters as well. Not long enough to warrant their own chapter, but still material that need not be ignored. Call it love, passion, eccentricity, or plain old crazy, but my dad always delivered in some way, shape, or form. Let's face it: how many 33 year old men are perfectly willing to spend more of their time talking about their father's exploits, rather than their own? People not even related to Wild Bill can't help but tell Wild Bill stories. Occasionally, things come full circle and a stranger will tell me a Wild Bill story, having no idea that Wild Bill was responsible for creating me as well the situation that resulted in the story.

Don't get me wrong, I have indeed stopped to ask myself, "Is this normal? Is it healthy to spend so much time talking about my father's antics?" Once, on a vacation, I turned to my good friend, Adam Milakofsky, and said, "Hey man, do you think I am telling too many stories? Do you think people get sick of me talking about my father?" Straight faced, he turned to me, "You kidding me? Wild Bill is the best part of this trip. Keep the stories coming." Here we were in Australia, one of the most beautiful places on earth, with plenty of opportunities to make our own stories, and my friends and I couldn't stop telling tales about Wild Bill. I've been told several times throughout my life to commit Wild Bill's legend to paper. This is my best attempt, and I only hope to do these stories, and my father, the justice they deserve.

For a little background, Drema and Wild Bill Caldwell have four children: Doreen, Billy, Scott, and me (Matt). Doreen is the oldest (now 48), Billy a few years behind, with Scott as third in the pecking order. I was born nine long years after Scott. My mom refers to me as her "oops" baby. If there is one trait that binds this family, it's our storytelling skills. Just as Italians are known for their food, Caldwells are known for their classic stories. We had the good fortune of growing up around my mother, who tells stories with the best. I believe her to be the architect that designed our storytelling abilities. She commands a room like no other. She is unparalleled in her ability to start a story, veer off to make a few additional points, and return from the wonderful detour to an extraordinary conclusion of the original story.

Each of the Caldwell children inherited different aspects of our mother's story telling persona. Scott has a very dry, straightforward approach, capable of knocking people off their chairs. His direct and concise way of articulating a story amazes people. Scott can easily pack more power into three words than I can in a paragraph. Doreen can be somewhat shy at times, but once she gets going, her energy is unstoppable. She could write her own chapter about her experience fighting a credit card bill in court with Wild Bill representing her as her lawyer. I would argue, however, that nobody tops my brother Billy. At Scott's 40th birthday party, I played the role of youngest sibling by being part moderator and part attention-grabber. Realizing this, my sister countered with a few Wild Bill specials of her own. Not one to be sidelined, my mother jumped in and one-upped the both of us. Then Billy brought the house down. It was the unmatched crescendo of the evening's performances, igniting the party and leaving the entire room in tears of laughter. We literally ended the "roast" because nobody could possibly follow Billy.

Given the delicate nuances of good storytelling, I worried when I began this project that something would be lost in translation in writing some of these tales. I feared I could never write something "eloquent" enough to do justice to the oral history of Wild Bill. Writing everything down, I reasoned, would strip away the energy and eccentricity that are integral parts of every Wild Bill classic.

Upon further reflection, I realized the only reason we are good storytellers is because we have good stories to tell. The material itself is what matters, not some magical storytelling ability that I believed my family was blessed with. In fact, my father isn't actually funny at all. The reason he is such a good source of story material is because he truly believes everything he does is perfectly normal, rational, and in no way whatsoever embarrassing to him, his family, or whatever poor souls happen to be stuck around him when he's in full "Wild Bill" mode. He can't even tell a good story. We have never sat around the campfire and been regaled with tales of the good ol' days by Wild Bill himself. Rather, he provides an endless source of material for the rest of us.

The Caldwells may make a marginal difference with their storytelling ability, but by now I've realized that anyone could tell these stories and they would still be funny. It is humbling to realize that my story telling abilities aren't worth anything compared to the actual substance of Wild Bill's antics, but this realization is what freed me up to actually write this book.

We have always discussed the need to write down these epic stories, and this is my best attempt. Whether or not this book ever gets published or gains any traction, my goal is to provide my family with memories of our father in written form. Not that I worry that we will ever stop telling these stories. That would be a long shot. I just doubt anyone can any ever replicate the man that is Wild Bill. I want to make sure all of our children, grandchildren, and right on down the Caldwell line, have something to reminisce about.

I also would like to mention that all proceeds of the book will be given to Wild Bill and Drema's grandkids, but only to be used for college. Cerina, Matthew, Mackenzie, James and Payton, sorry, you have no choice. You are going to college. I can't guarantee it will be a lot of money; maybe most outsiders will consider us just some whack job family. However, given that the Kardashians can make millions off some ridiculous TV show, we may have a few bucks to give you for college. I am sure Wild Bill's stories have a little more substance than shopping in NYC or fighting at some nightclub. I guess we will find out.

I do have to give credit to the origins of the Wild Bill moniker. The family actually didn't give it to him. In fact, it came from a classmate that I haven't spoken to in years. Unfortunately, I can't recall his name, but we were in the same platoon one summer during our military training at West Point. On Sundays, my dad would drive out to our training facility (called Camp Buckner) and bring a six foot hero sandwich to all of us cadets. Many of the senior officers who were supervising us didn't approve of his visits, but then again, Wild Bill could care less about West Point protocol. During one visit, this fine soldier commented, "Here comes that Wild Bill again." Remarkably, our family hadn't thought of the nickname in the past, but in that instant the name was born.

I also owe a special thanks to Laura Dodd, Chris Boggiano, Neil Prakash, and Matt Keane. Laura, we became friends recently and after I found out you were an author yourself, I immediately put you to work. Your advice and guidance along the way was imperative to get this book off the ground. Chris, you were the first person I approached to help edit. I was at a point where I was staring at a computer screen for months and really needed someone to help put some structure to the book. As always, you stepped up to the plate and helped out a friend. What you do for your friends is truly admirable. Neil, you really helped me think big picture. You gave tremendous advice about addressing major parts of the book and what sections to expand upon and what parts to make more concise. I still recall one Sunday afternoon where we spent hours speaking passionately about the Wild Bill stories as if he was some fictional character.

Matt, I can't thank you enough. I appreciate you spending many hours reviewing the material so I don't have to actually pay an editor or publisher. Not to mention another trait I have picked up from my father...Saving money at all costs! Your grammatical changes were imperative to the flow of the book. Additionally, it was great to have someone review the book that has never met Wild Bill. Your objective advice was instrumental. Finally, I also would like to thank Mike Murphy and Bill Doherty for helping me develop the cover, which for those who know Wild Bill, could not be more illustrative of his personality.

Oh and one last thing, Dad: no more complaining that your kids never do anything for you. This book should shut you up (at least for a little while)!

1 KOSOVO

As a brand new U.S. Army second lieutenant, reporting to your first duty station is a relatively terrifying experience. Here you are: some 22 year old college kid—in my case a West Point graduate—and you are expected to lead a group of 20-50 soldiers, who have all been in the Army longer than you. The young privates can't believe they are the same age as you, yet they still have to call you "Sir." At the other end of the spectrum, there are sergeants old enough to be your father, and they also work for you. Even worse, your fellow officers (who one would hope might be on your side) view you as an embarrassment waiting to happen;

preferring to keep a safe distance until you prove whether you will sink or swim. In short, you are at the bottom of a very deep barrel.

My first duty station was Vilseck, Germany, where I joined the historic 1st Infantry Division. After graduating from West Point and completing Armor Officer Basic Course at Fort Knox, I reported to Vilseck on February 7, 2003. A few months earlier, in the fall of 2002, my unit deployed to Kosovo, a province of the former Yugoslavia, which had been in a state of persistent ethnic conflict since the country's breakup. After the ethnic cleansing, orchestrated by Serbian President Slobodan Milosevic, the U.S. began a bombing campaign in 1999 under my old friend, President Bill Clinton (whom my father had connected me with several years earlier—see Chapter 3). U.S. troops had been deployed to Kosovo since that time, and my unit was attempting to keep the peace among the locals. After a couple weeks in Germany, I was informed that I would be joining them in Kosovo for the remainder of the deployment. At that point, it was time to call my family and inform them of this new development.

After all my West Point training and speculating about deploying for a real-world mission, my time was finally here. I proceeded to call my mother, sister, and brothers, who were all deeply concerned about my safety. I vividly remember calling my cousin, April Mingione, and the phone falling completely silent. I could hear her choking up on the other end of the line. I tried to explain that this was just a peacekeeping mission and there was nothing to worry about, but my argument fell on deaf ears. In an era so soon after September 11th, any deployment was a scary thought for my family, who otherwise had little interaction with the military.

While nowhere near as dangerous as Iraq or Afghanistan, Kosovo was still considered a war zone. Given the uncertainty of the mission, my family didn't know what to expect. As a cadet, the possibility of going to war was always in the back of everyone's mind, but it was such an abstract concept that no one spent much time thinking about it. It didn't help that I entered West Point during the relatively peaceful era of the late 1990's, but graduated and commissioned just eight months after the 9/11 terrorist attacks. When I started at the Academy, I don't think my family believed that me going to war was a realistic possibility. We were obviously all very bad at predicting the future. Even as a peacekeeping mission, Kosovo was my first real test as a young Army officer.

I called my father last. One of the first times I realized my dad wasn't quite normal was when he snuck me into a Yankee game for one of my earlier birthdays. At the time, I remember thinking that we were doing the impossible. It was my first glimpse of Wild Bill's knack for overcoming the impossible. Little did I know what I would encounter later in my life.

After a little small talk, which I know he thoroughly despises, and sensing that he wanted me to get to the point, I broke the news about Kosovo. I was expecting Wild Bill to express the same concerns as my other relatives; instead he had one simple question—"What about your birthday?" I was utterly confused. "Excuse me, dad"? To which he responded, "Ya know, your birthday is in two months. I want to come see you." At first I thought he simply didn't understand the circumstances, so I tried to explain a second time, "Dad, you see, maybe you're not getting what I'm saying. I am not going to be in Germany. I am going to be in Kosovo." To which he responded, in typical New York fashion, "What the hell is Kosovo?"

After some explanation, including a short history lesson on the region and why U.S. forces were deployed there, he finally said, "Well great, I'll just come to Kosovo." Laughing to myself, I explained why he couldn't just visit Kosovo: it was a third world country; it actually wasn't even recognized as a country at the time; the only airport there was controlled by United Nations peacekeepers; it was dangerous to travel there as a civilian; the fact that you couldn't exactly hop on an American Airlines flight from JFK to Kosovo; and so on. The most perplexing aspect was that I couldn't wrap my mind around why it was such a big deal to see me on this particular birthday. I was twenty-two years old; not ten, or eighteen, or even twenty-one. His response to me: "Bull Fucking Shit. I will be there."

As I mentioned earlier, my dad spent 35 years in the NYPD, eventually reaching the rank of Captain and also President of the Superior Officer Association for the housing police department (all ranks above patrolmen – Captains, Lieutenants, Sergeants, etc). This was a police union for the housing police. So, why would this man have any appreciation for things like international treaties, the Geneva Conventions, or the rule of law in general? His mentality has always been very simple: if there is a will, there is a way. Dad always made a point to do something special for his kids on their birthday, but visiting a war zone was about as possible as going for a weekend trip to the moon.

Given my father's insistence that he could visit Kosovo, I emailed one of my best friends, Jon Monken, who was already deployed with our battalion and said: "Monks, any chance my dad could get to Kosovo." I am sure he had the same reaction as I did, but he knew my family was eccentric, so he tried to explain to me the difficulties and dangers of trying to get there, just as I had tried to explain to my father. He laughed it off and rattled off several of the same reasons why Wild Bill could never show up, but Jon thought it was a very nice "gesture." I tried relaying Jon's logic to Wild Bill, hoping a second opinion would help clarify the situation. I don't think he listened to a word I said.

During deployments, soldiers work seven days a week with no days off for holidays or weekends. As a civilian it sounds rough, but there's usually nothing else to do, so working 10 to 12 hours per day quickly becomes your new "normal." The repetitive routine becomes oddly reassuring at a time when so many other things in a soldier's life are out of whack. One of the interesting side effects of the monotony is that it's very common to lose track of the days of the week. After all, if every day is the same, there isn't really a difference between a Saturday and a Tuesday.

April 30th, 2003 was just another day in Kosovo. I had arrived in the region about two months earlier and was still the most junior ranking officer in the battalion. I was called into work early that morning, unexpectedly, and had actually forgotten that it was my birthday. So there I was as a fresh new lieutenant doing all of the things West Point had prepared me to do: getting coffee for senior officers, hunting for coffee filters, and emptying the trash around our unit's operations center—basically all the things the new guy gets stuck with until he proves himself.

In the middle of this morning routine, a sergeant entered the building and said, "Is there a Lieutenant Matt Caldwell here?" I thought to myself, they must have the wrong guy. Nobody here really knows my name yet. I reluctantly raised my hand thinking the Sergeant must have had the wrong name. "Sir, please come outside. Someone needs to speak to you." I started to get nervous as a million things ran through my mind: "Is this a setup? Are they messing with the new guy? Maybe even the Serbians or Albanians are in on this prank?"

I timidly walked outside. I then heard something that I will never forget for as long as I live. I couldn't see anyone at first because it came from around the corner of the building, but it was an unmistakably recognizable voice: "You think I wouldn't see my fucking son for his 23rd birthday!!!" It hit me all at once. Holy shit—he actually pulled it off, Wild Bill was in Kosovo. I can't describe how surreal the entire encounter felt. I was standing there, in a combat zone a million miles from home, with my M-9 pistol in a holster at my side, wearing my army fatigues, and staring back at me was my father with his NYPD hat, a cigar clenched in his teeth, wearing a Cohiba t-shirt and khaki shorts.

I couldn't believe my eyes. First of all, I couldn't come to terms with the fact that my father was actually in a war zone. For those who haven't been deployed, envision a beat up town with bullet holes and shrapnel dotting the walls of every building. War zones typically include soldiers carrying rifles and pistols, Humvees and other military vehicles buzzing in all directions, raw sewage and trash everywhere, and the occasional landmine. In

Kosovo, there were the local Albanians and Serbians—skinny, hungry, cold, miserable, and genuinely worried someone was going to kill them at any moment. There were also US soldiers walking around in their battle dress uniform. It was a pretty clear divide. Additionally, our base had roughly 400 male soldiers and not a single female. Now, try to imagine just how much a guy in shorts and a t-shirt sticks out. I thought to myself, "If I were traveling to a war zone, would I wear shorts and a t-shirt? Should I make the slightest effort to try to fit in?" Wild Bill clearly could not be bothered with asking himself such questions before boarding a plane at JFK airport.

Again, the 23rd birthday aspect raced through my mind. As if it was a special milestone? I should have seen this moment coming during that pre-deployment phone call to my Dad. He said it like "of course, I would visit you in Kosovo for 23. Doesn't everyone do that?" Any sane person would have certainly made a different set of decisions leading up to this moment, but not Wild Bill. To him it was quite simple: He wanted to visit his son on his birthday and nothing in the world would stop him from doing just that. Everything else—the 5000 mile trip, the war zone, the military—these were just minor details.

Now, my dad is probably the cheapest person alive. He grew up in a relatively poor family. During my childhood we lived pretty comfortably, but to hear him tell it, we were living in the great depression. His first step on his journey to Kosovo was getting the cheapest possible flight to anywhere in central Europe, which happened to be Zurich, Switzerland (about 1000 miles from Kosovo). As best I can tell, he didn't really have a plan after Zurich. One of Wild Bill's best traits is that he just assumes he will figure out a way to succeed and never take no for an answer. He thrives in situations where most normal people would think a few steps ahead and be terrified that they had no plan of what to do next.

So, after landing, he roamed the airport to figure out his next move. He spotted a uniformed United Nations border patrol officer and recognized a golden opportunity. Many people don't realize this, but being a cop is like being part of a legal international mafia. Cops universally take care of one another. So Wild Bill struck up a conversation with the international border patrol police and convinced them that he was a part of a police program that was sending New York City police officers to Kosovo to train the local police. Now the piece about the police program was technically true, in that such a program did actually exist. The key detail he left out was that he was in no way affiliated with that particular program. I later found out that he had applied for the program at some point, but had been rejected. Why would an international police training program want an out of shape 60 year old retired NYPD captain?

After convincing the border patrol agents that he was part of the police program, he showed them his badge and some paperwork he had about the training program. He went on to explain that he had missed his flight from Zurich to Kosovo and was wondering if they might be able to help him out. As luck would have it, there was actually a UN flight headed to Kosovo that night and all of the border patrol officers were accompanying the flight. A few hours later, Wild Bill was on a UN charter flight to Kosovo!

My dad has never been the most book-smart person in the world, but his street-smarts are second to none. In-flight to

Kosovo, he realized there was no way he was going to be able to pull off the same feat on his way back home. Why would a guy who had just arrived in Kosovo (after missing his flight) need a trip home only two days later (after missing another flight)? He knew the story would be too suspicious to be believable. So, somewhere over the Adriatic Sea, he walked up to the cockpit and said to the pilot, "Listen pal, I am not supposed to be here. I am just surprising my son for his 23rd birthday. Any chance you can throw me on the manifest for your return trip?"

I would give just about anything to have been a fly on the wall for that conversation. I can just picture the pilot flying an official UN plane and some bear of a man, not only in civilian clothes, but in shorts and t-shirt, just strolls into the cockpit asking for a flight back to Switzerland in a few days. It was like he was hitchhiking across the globe, but the best part was that the pilot told him it wouldn't be a problem and had him added to the manifest. Wild Bill already had a flight back to Zurich before he even landed!

So that's how Wild Bill got into the country of Kosovo. His next mission was to find someone in the Pristina airport who spoke English. When I refer to an airport in Kosovo, don't think it is anything like what you might see in the United States. In 2003, Pristina Airport was a small air base that generally only accepted military flights into and out of the country.

Once he tracked down the guy who spoke English, he had this gentleman call each and every U.S. military base in the country, because of course he had no idea which one I was actually stationed at. After eventually finding out that Camp MaGrath was the home of Lieutenant Matt Caldwell, he was informed that civilians were not allowed inside the base camp. Furthermore, he would need a special pass from the embassy to leave the airport.

Again, never one to take no for an answer, my father instructed the soldier who answered the phone at my base to put the "head guy on the line." My battalion commander (who ran our base camp), Lieutenant Colonel Jeffrey Kulp, spoke to my dad and was amazed that this man was in Kosovo and had found us. Once he had Colonel Kulp on the phone, my dad explained that he was in the "police training program" and that he just wanted to swing by the base to say hello to his son. Although my commander instantly knew something was fishy, he begrudgingly agreed to allow my father to come on the base. Before my dad hung up, he requested that my Colonel not say anything because he wanted to surprise his son for his birthday.

As an adult, can you imagine having your father tell your boss (and not a typical boss—a Lieutenant Colonel in the Army) that he wanted to come by the office to surprise you for your birthday? I was so embarrassed when I later heard about the phone call. After I met my dad, the Lieutenant Colonel called me into his office. He said, "Lieutenant, I have been in the Army for almost 20 years, and I have never seen anything like this. I know he claims he is in some police program, but I know something is up. It's ok for you to see him, but he can't spend the night."

I took my orders and then grabbed my father and brought him to where I was living, which was basically a tiny trailer. Once we were alone, I asked, "Dad, how the hell did you pull this off?" Straight faced, he pulled out a grainy black and white printout from Yahoo with a map of Europe and driving directions from Zurich to Kosovo. Circling all of Europe with his finger, he said, "I figured if I got here that I could figure out a way to get across the Mediterranean to Kosovo." The general area where Kosovo was located was highlighted in yellow. At the time, Kosovo wasn't even a recognized country, so there was no mention of it on the map. To this day, my father doesn't use the internet. The image of my computer-illiterate 60 year old father, standing there with a "map" of Europe on a sheet of paper that I am sure he just had someone else print out for him on their home printer, will forever be etched in my mind.

After the initial excitement and his abbreviated explanation of how he got to Kosovo, Wild Bill got down to business. He pulled out my recent tax return, which had been sent to my mother's house. He started asking me questions about how and why I filed it the way I did. In a span of 30 seconds he transformed from Wild Bill, the rogue cop wandering around Kosovo, to my stern accountant. I couldn't believe what was happening—my father was standing in my Army trailer in Kosovo and lecturing me about my tax returns. Some things never change. It's almost like he was so cheap that he came to Kosovo to straighten out my taxes for me.

After the tax prep discussion, I went to the chow hall for breakfast and met another great friend and roommate at the time, Chris Boggiano. Chris is one of the smartest and funniest Army officers I have ever met. He has a rare combination of high intelligence with a great sense of humor and common sense. One of the many qualities I admire about Chris is his ability to remain unemotional and rational in any situation, no matter what is thrown at him, or shot at him for that matter. When I told him my father was not only in Kosovo, but in our trailer at that moment, his jaw dropped and he just sat there staring at me with his fork held halfway to his mouth in complete disbelief. He was totally speechless. This is a guy who always has something witty or sarcastic to say no matter the situation, and he was mute. Completely dumbfounded.

After the shock passed, I brought Chris to the trailer to meet my father. Chris also has an eccentric Jersey City cop father himself. We would trade "war stories" all the time about growing up with our dads, but I think this finally settled the debate over which of our fathers was crazier. My dad introduced himself to Chris and immediately told him to get his suitcase that he had left at the front gate of our camp. For security reasons, the soldier at the gate would not let Wild Bill take his bag onto the base. My father was on my base for five minutes and he was already running the place and giving Chris orders. The best part is that Chris didn't ask any questions. He immediately left to get the bag.

Another interesting aspect of this absurd story is that Wild Bill never told anyone back home that he had left for Kosovo. Given that the Caldwell family talks to each other every day, the phones were buzzing when Wild Bill went missing. From the day I got my first cell phone, I've routinely received voicemails from family members with some version of, "Is this Matthew? Are you alive? I haven't heard from you." My mom and dad talk most days even though they are technically separated—a unique situation that I will address in a later chapter. Needless to say, I just accept that my family isn't normal and that everyone in the family is extremely involved in everyone else's life.

So I brought my father to our community phone center where soldiers could make calls home to the United States (thanks to the USO and other services that are so great for American soldiers). Given that I had just only arrived in Kosovo a couple of months earlier, I had not yet made any calls home. My first call was to my brother Scott who was working in New York City. Scott answered the phone and could hear the excitement in my voice—even though we had gone the longest stretch of time in our lives without talking, he knew that something had to be going on to get me so excited. He could sense it in my voice.

After exchanging pleasantries, I said to Scott, "Hold on one second. Someone wants to say hello." Doing his best Robin Williams impersonation from the movie Good Morning Vietnam, my father grabs the phone and screams into it, "Gooooddd Morning Kosovo!!!!" And then he just dropped the phone on the table and stepped away. I pick it up to hear my brother say, "You have got to be kidding me. Is this a conference call or something?" I responded, "No Scott. He is standing next to me. In Kosovo."

Now, my father is like a little kid. You have to keep an eye on him, if you don't want him to wander off and get into trouble. As I began explaining the situation to my brother, I looked up and realized that my father had left our phone booth and was talking to a soldier who was on the phone in the booth next to us. My dad has no respect for social etiquette so he was oblivious to the concept that the soldier might be talking to his girlfriend or mother back home. He also didn't understand that each soldier was allotted only 15 minutes for each phone call.

As a typical New Yorker, my dad just interrupted the soldier's phone call and struck up a conversation. Realizing this, I put my brother on hold and tried to pull my father away from the soldier, so the poor guy could finish his call. I said to him, "Dad, leave the kid alone. He only has so much time on the phone." Much to my surprise, the soldier stands up and is wearing an NYPD hat and shirt. He says to me, "I know Bill. I let him in at the front gate. Who are you?" I almost lost it. My dad had already made friends on the base. I had been there two months and people were asking me how I knew Wild Bill, as if I was the outsider.

After all of the excitement had passed, I explained to my father that he could not sleep on the base. Although my battalion commander had agreed to let him onto the base, he did not want to be too welcoming because he was afraid that soldiers' wives would hear about Wild Bill and try to make the trip out to Kosovo to see their husbands. The result was that he could come to visit during the day, but he needed to find a place to stay among the locals at night.

I was a little more than worried and had no idea what to do with him. However, as my siblings can attest, whenever we start to worry about dad, he gives us a look that essentially says, "Leave me the hell alone. You don't know anything." In this case, that familiar look was followed by, "I found this place, didn't I? I will find a place to sleep too." So my dad proceeded to the front gate and stopped one of the platoons that was about to leave on a patrol. He then convinces them to give him a ride into town. The patrol took him to a random local house and Wild Bill offered the man of the house 50 Euros to stay the night. Being a poor country, that was a substantial amount of money in Kosovo, so the homeowner excitedly accepted the cash and welcomed him inside. Leaving nothing to chance, Wild Bill arranged for the same platoon to pick him up in the morning and bring him back to our base camp. He carried on this routine for three days until he worked his way back to Pristina Airport, met up with his friends from the UN, and hitched a ride on a flight back to Switzerland.

So my first of many, my apologies to the countless unnamed souls in Kosovo who were harassed so Wild Bill could visit his son on his 23rd birthday.

2 IRAQ

I returned to Germany from Kosovo in July 2003. America had invaded Iraq earlier that spring, and as a result, I found out before I even got back home to Germany that our unit would deploy to Iraq in early 2004. Wild Bill managed to visit me on my 23rd birthday in Kosovo, but fortunately he did not try to do the same for my 24th birthday in Iraq. My family is very thankful he didn't try to outdo himself, as it likely would have been a suicide mission. Unbelievably, I actually did have to talk him out of trying to come visit me, and I wasn't entirely sure until my birthday had passed if he had actually heeded my advice to not come to Iraq. Although he stayed at home, that doesn't mean he didn't find a way to have an impact on our mission in Iraq from all the way back in New York City.

When we first got to Iraq, there was a lot of talk in the media about how American troops were not properly equipped for the war. The U.S. military had done a marvelous job preparing for the invasion of Iraq, but it did not expect to be stuck in Iraq conducting patrols and fighting an insurgency which was in full swing by the time I arrived in the country in February 2004. As part of a multi-year game of catch-up, there were delays in getting vital equipment to the soldiers on the front lines.

Given how quickly the war progressed from an invasion to counter-insurgency, many units did not bring their heavily armored vehicles or tanks, because they simply weren't a good fit for the Army's new mission in Iraq. Heavily armored tanks keep soldiers safe, but they also prevent interaction with the local populace, and create a lot of aggravated locals the same way a bull might upset the owner of a china shop. At the same time, the Humvee trucks that most units used for patrols had little to no armor at all, and most roadside bombs would rip right through their thin canvas or fiberglass doors.

With all of the media coverage concerning equipment shortfalls, Wild Bill was not content to stand pat and wait for some bureaucrat to deliver the right equipment to protect his son. Instead, he organized a collection in New York City, encouraging retired police officers to donate their old bullet proof vests. After collecting over one thousand vests in a period of a few months, he shipped them to me in Iraq. His idea was that we could line the floors and doors of our trucks with them to add some protection for me and my fellow soldiers. By the time the vests arrived, however, my unit had already received "up-armored" Humvees with thick metal doors, so there was really no longer a need for any additional protection the old police vests would provide.

I may not be as crazy as my father, but in this instance I wanted to take advantage of this opportunity. Rather than letting the vests sit around and collect dust, I decided to distribute them to the local Iraqi police officers who we worked within our unit's area of operations. This not only provided them protection, but also helped to build a great rapport between my platoon and the local villagers. In a way, it was a lot like my dad giving out NYPD hats and police shirts to soldiers during his field trip to Kosovo.

Throughout my year in Iraq, we worked closely with the Iraqi Army and Police to help them provide security in different neighborhoods in our sector. It was always a challenge to build trust because so few of them spoke English, and none of my soldiers spoke Arabic. However, giving them vests that had been shipped from the United States was a very effective way of saying that we saw them as allies and cared about their safety. It fostered a tremendous amount of goodwill and deepened our ties with the local populace. At the same time, it was hysterical to see Iraqi police officer wearing bulletproof vests with "NYPD" printed across the front. Wild Bill struck again winning hearts and minds.

After handing out the vests, I didn't think I would hear much else about it from either Iraqis or Americans. What I didn't realize was that the public relations team in my battalion had taken several pictures of these Iraqi police officers hard at work. At the end of each day, the officers in charge of the various sections of our battalion would brief our commander about the day's activities. Lieutenant Colonel Jeffrey Kulp, the same battalion commander who had met Wild Bill in Kosovo and allowed him onto our base about a year and half earlier, was still commanding the battalion.

One evening during the update briefing, a slide popped up that showed the pictures of the Iraqi police officers wearing NYPD police vests. Lieutenant Colonel Kulp interrupted the briefer, "Wait, what the hell are the Iraqi police doing wearing vests that say NYPD on them?" The captain giving the briefing responded, "Yes, well, Lieutenant Caldwell's father sent them over from New York." With a straight face, my colonel responded, "Is he coming to Iraq too?"

Only Wild Bill. Lieutenant Colonel Jeffrey Kulp, I apologize for giving you one more thing to worry about while trying to fight a war.

Email to Neil Prakash

Neil was one of the editors I mentioned at the beginning of the book. I served with him in the 1st Infantry Division and he has heard many Wild Bill stories throughout the years. When I mentioned to Neil about writing the book, he forwarded the email below that I sent him while he was serving in Afghanistan. I thought I would give the reader a live representation of Wild Bill, so I left the email in its original form:

So the other day there was a reported "gunman" at Northwestern law school. Within five minutes, I see the caller ID on my cell "Wild Bill." In this digital age with internet and social media, which my father doesn't use, it still amazes me how this man gets information quicker than anyone else. I answer the phone and the following conversation occurs:

> WB: Are you at that fucking Rubloff Hall? (Rubloff is the name of one of the buildings at the law school).
> MC: No pop.
> WB: Well there is a guy with a gun there.
> MC: I know dad, we were all informed.
> WB: Do you need help?
> MC: No, I think we are good.
> WB: Well don't try to be a fucking hero. You have done enough of that bullshit already.
> MC: (holding my dying laughter) Yes Pop.
> WB: Why are you being so short with me?

MC: I am not; I am just in a group meeting.

WB: I thought you just said you weren't at that Rubloff building.

MC: I am not. I am actually at the business school which is at a different location.

WB: Jesus, you are always getting fresh with me. This fucking JBL program is more confusing every day. Make sure you call your mother. (He calls the graduate program I am in "JBL." In fact, I am attending a JD/MBA program. And as a first year in law school, we are called "1L's." So I think he just shortened the whole thing.

MC: Pop, I am fine. Can I call you later?

He then proceeds to hang up. I think we were close to one minute anyway on the cell phone. My dad hates to go over one minute on cell phones because he doesn't want to get charged on the second minute without using the whole minute. Despite the fact that I have added him as a friend on Verizon and all our calls are free. He doesn't believe me.

3 BILL CLINTON

When I was younger, every year my father would take me to a national police conference. He was one of a handful of police officers that represented New York City at the convention. One year when I was 12 years old, President Bill Clinton spoke at the convention. He was trying to pass a piece of legislation and needed to get the cops to vote in support of the particular bill.

The morning that my dad found out about the speech, he immediately woke me up and asked, "Do you have a suit?" Implying that most young adults travel with suits. Not long after, I arrived at the President's speech in a pair of jeans and a collared shirt, the best I could do on such short notice. The room was fairly small, everyone was dressed in business attire, and I was 12, so needless to say I did not need any help standing out. This was only the beginning.

Even as a young kid, there were moments where I knew that my father was not a typical dad, much less a normal person. Most kids can go a pretty long time not recognizing their parents' quirks because they don't have any other parents as a basis of comparison. Still, there were just too many odd moments in the life of a Caldwell child. These were the kind of moments where I would have a wrenching pain in my stomach and a burning desire to find the nearest hole in the ground so I could crawl into it. Such events almost always centered on my father's complete lack of etiquette, protocol, fear of social awkwardness, or sense of embarrassment.

In this particular situation, I found myself sitting in the front row with Governor Mario Cuomo, Governor Christine Whitman, and Mayor Rudy Giuliani. I had no special access pass to be there, although everyone apparently assumed that I did. After he quickly ushered me to the front of the room, my dad told me, "sit here, read this magazine, don't talk to anyone, and make it look like you belong." I did exactly what he said and nobody questioned whether I should be sitting there, or who I belonged to. Everyone must have assumed that I was the President's nephew or a relative of some other important person. I vividly remember these high ranking politicians talking to each other and saying, "Who is this kid?" I kept my mouth shut and no one said a word to me, so I was left alone until President Clinton approached the podium to give his speech.

It was a phenomenal speech and an amazing experience to be in such close proximity to the President. I recall thinking to myself, halfway through the speech, that things always had a way of working out when it came to my father's shenanigans.

Except he wasn't quite done in this particular instance. During the President's speech, I heard someone from the back room, "Psssst....pssst." Wild Bill is the only person who could be speaking in such a small room during an address from the leader of the free world. After hearing the noise, I looked over my shoulder to the back of the room to see him standing with an old "throw away" disposable camera trying to take a picture. Never satisfied, he wanted me to stand up in the front row during the speech so he could take the picture. The man is completely irrepressible. Even as a 12 year old, I understood the gravity of the situation and I could not believe what was happening. He was asking me to stand up so he could get a clear a picture with the President in the background.

Mortified, I quickly turned back around, ignored him, and pretended I did not know who he was or what was going on. Despite years of embarrassment, one thing I never seemed to learn was that my father did not care what other people thought and would not stop until he got what he wanted. In this case, he wanted a picture of me standing in front of the President during his speech.

I then felt a woman tap me on the shoulder. "Kid, you might as well stand up, because he won't stop back there." He had everyone from the back of the audience tap the shoulder of the person in front of them to pass forward the message for me to stand up. There was no ignoring him this time. If I didn't stand up, he would just keep escalating things until he got his picture. So yes, I stood up in the middle of the President's speech and he snapped a picture.

You would think he would have been happy with that, but Wild Bill wanted more. Immediately after the speech, my father grabbed me and we followed the President to the bathroom. Yes, the bathroom. Again, no secret service or security stopped us or questioned who we were. Wild Bill oozes confidence that allows him to convince others that everything he does is somehow ok and they shouldn't question whatever he's doing. Waiting for the President to exit the bathroom and then cornering him in the hallway, my father said, "Mr. President (I was surprised my dad even knew to say that), would you take a picture with my son?" The consummate politician, Bill Clinton responded, "Well yes, of course."

The President had no idea what he was getting into. With my dad's little throw away camera, he forgot he had to turn the wheel so that he could take another picture. For what was the most awkward minute of my life, I stood posed shaking the President's hand outside of a men's bathroom, while my father couldn't get his camera to work. I remember President Clinton awkwardly laughing and saying, "Ya know, I do need to get going." My dad responded, "Nah hold on. I'll get this in a second." He spoke to the President as if he was just another one of his buddies down at the police precinct.

He eventually figured out what was wrong, turned the wheel, and got his picture. I couldn't believe my father told the President to "hold on." Furthermore, I couldn't believe that it worked and the President followed Wild Bill's instructions. At the end of the day though, I have a picture with President Bill Clinton. Sorry for the hassle, Mr. President.

4 POPE

Wow. Where do I start with this one? It sounds like a bad joke: The Pope, a NYPD Police Captain, and a kid in a wheelchair walk into Madison Square Garden...

For a little background, my brother Scott suffered a terrible injury while visiting my mother's family in Ohio when he was eight years old. During the visit, Scott got off the beaten path on my grandmother's property and stepped on a live power line that was lying on the ground and was electrocuted. My other brother Billy saved his life by pulling him off the power line, performing mouth to mouth, and summoning my cousin to get my father. Ironically, Billy had just watched a mouth to mouth class on TV a few weeks prior, which helped him while Scott lay on the ground unconscious. I enclosed an article from the Staten Island Advance about the incident in the pictures section.

Upon arrival, Wild Bill grabbed Scott, trucked through a shallow river, and rushed him to the nearby hospital. The doctors at the hospital told my family that there was almost no chance that Scott would survive. He remained in a coma and on a respirator for a few days. My family started to lose faith and was preparing for a life without Scott. Despite what we were told from the hospital, our relatives in the area questioned why we were at this particular hospital when there was a better burn center not too far away.

The doctors, however, assured us that we were at the right place. That wasn't enough for Wild Bill. As my sister recalls, Wild Bill grabbed one of the doctors, brought him in a room and threw him up against the wall and screamed in his face, 'If this was your son, what burn center would he be at?" Of course under duress, the doctor admitted that Scott should be at the other hospital. I guess the hospital was hoping to collect some medical bills while Scott remained on a respirator, but rest assured, we would find the best hospital for my brother. Wild Bill was in charge.

Miraculously, Scott awoke from the coma a few days after arriving at the new burn center. My mother recalls being in the waiting room and the alarms started going off alerting the nurses and doctor to Scott's room as there was an emergency. Still, my family was then told that he would lose his foot and because of the nature of the injury that he would have to relearn many of the basic functions he learned as a child. Although it was a terrible outcome, it was obviously better than death, and Scott did eventually make a full recovery.

After months of therapy in Ohio, Scott finally returned to New York. He was in numerous newspapers and the local little league had a welcome home party for him. It was a very difficult time for my brother because he needed to relearn all the basic functions in life - talking, walking, jogging, throwing a football, etc. These things came back to him quickly, but it was still a long struggle. He was in therapy for almost a year and it was a very tough time for my family.

During this time, Pope John Paul II was visiting Central Park
in 1979. Additionally, he was conducting a mass in Madison
Square Garden to bless the city of New York. Did you think Wild
Bill was going to miss this opportunity?

Somehow, my father organized for the Pope to bring my
brother on the stage of Madison Square Garden to bless him in
front of the crowd. I don't even know how you get to the Pope,
but my dad did. He worked out a deal where the Pope would bless
my brother Scott on stage in front of thousands of worshipers. It's
almost ridiculous to even write this. We are talking about one of
the most famous people ever and Wild Bill somehow got my
brother in front of him. If I were reading this, I wouldn't believe
this stuff. That's one of the reasons I tried to include as many
pictures as possible.

Well, the Pope did attempt to take my brother on the stage.
Again, my dad had one of his sons (in this case Scott) in the first
row during the mass - it's one of his favorite moves. Scott was in a
wheelchair when the Pope walked over to bring him on stage at the
Garden. My brother, however, got nervous and refused to go with
him. As an eight year old, I am sure having an older stranger

trying to bring you on stage in front of thousands of people was a terrifying experience. Even though Scott survived a near death experience, I think my dad was ready to kill him. Regardless, I have to give him credit for arranging the deal in the first place.

My father once said to me, "Son, when faced with adversity, you must turn the situation into an opportunity." I can't think of many other quotes that sum up my dad like this one. He thrives on crises and getting things done for his children. In this instance, my family was suffering through a very tough time as they watched Scott experience such a traumatic event and tried to guide him to recovery. It was moving to have my dad reach out to one of the most famous people of the last century and get him to bless my brother on the stage of the Garden. Taking "advantage" of my brother's horrific accident, he jumped on the opportunity to get my brother to meet the Pope. He always figures out a way to make things better.

When I speak to my brother about it today, he is still in shock. He doesn't remember much from the accident, but he sure remembers Madison Square Garden. Of course now he regrets getting scared, but at the time, he didn't realize the significance of the opportunity. All he knew was my dad was yelling at him "Get your ass up there" and Scott was terrified of the guy with the funny hat. Scott laughs when he recalls the story, but it was a monumental time in his recovery. He realized that despite everything he was going through, Wild Bill and the family were not only at his side, but also working deals with the Pope to make him happy. Like many other things my dad does, Wild Bill is not very emotional about it. He just does it. I have asked him about the Pope meeting and he said, "I just started calling everyone - the mayor, police commissioner, UN - until they gave me the right answer."

Wild Bill and the Pope. Sorry for inconvenience, Pope John Paul II.

The Water Cooler

The was another classic Wild Bill story that I didn't think warranted its own chapter, but I wanted to include it in the book. Given that I grew up close to West Point, I used to bring home cadets on the limited weekends we had off. On one such weekend, I brought home my roommate, Josh Minney and a few other cadets. When we arrived, Josh saw my father running around the yard doing his usual: picking up twigs, dog shit, and anything else that drove him crazy. I went inside, gave my mother a hug and kiss, and got ready for the night. If there is one thing about West Point cadets, we are very efficient in maximizing our off time and trying to get in as much fun as possible before going back to the confines of the Academy.

After a night partying around New York City, my buddies and I returned home to my mother's house. As good soldiers, we figured we would each drink a glass of water in order to hydrate for the next day. My mother had a water cooler in her house filled with cold, fresh Poland Spring water. At least so we thought.

We each took a few sips of water and all looked startled. Something didn't taste right. With that, Josh Minney broke out in laughter. We were all wondering what was wrong, but he couldn't catch his breath to tell us his realization. After a few moments, he finally revealed the content of his laughter. Josh commented, "Matt, when we arrived at your house before, I noticed your dad running around the yard. I also noticed that he had a Poland Spring jug with him. I thought it was rather interesting and I was wondering why he walking around with the jug. I then saw him fill the jug with hose water! I thought to myself that he must have some reason, but never imagined that he was using the hose water for the actual water cooler."

At that point, I never saw West Point cadets laugh so hard in my life. We were besides ourselves that Wild Bill had the audacity to fill the jug with hose water in order to not have to purchase a new jug of Poland Spring.

5 US OPEN – PART I

Wild Bill knows nothing about golf nor has he ever swung a club. What he does know though is that his sons enjoy playing. After moving to Bethpage, NY, in 2001, my father noticed there was a popular golf course in his new neighborhood. For all those non-golfers out there, Bethpage is one of the nicest public golf courses in the country, so much so that the US Open has been played there a few times over the past decade. Naturally, I get a call from him on a Friday night, "So you want to play the Bethpage golf course tomorrow?"

I quickly assumed that he didn't know what he was talking about and fell into the same trap that always gets me by trying to explain to him why we couldn't do something: "Dad, you don't just show up at Bethpage golf course. There is a formal reservation system and its one of the most difficult public courses to get a reservation." I explained to him that people park their cars overnight on Friday nights in order to be there early to get a tee time on Saturday morning. Additionally, the course would be hosting the US Open the following year (June 2002), so reservations would even be more difficult than usual because of the increased publicity for the course.

My father responds with, "I'll call you in the morning with a tee time. Grab your brothers and get out here when I call you." I told him that if he was miraculously able to get us a reservation that we would need a couple hours to make the drive out to Bethpage. In typical fashion, he woke me up the next morning with a 5:30 am phone call and a set of instructions, "Get out of bed. I got us a 7:00 am tee time." Off to the races we go. I flew out of bed, grabbed my brothers, and we sped out to Long Island to get there in time.

We arrived at the golf course a few minutes late for our tee time. You can probably guess where this is going, but needless to say that golf is a game with a certain etiquette and protocol along with a large number of rules that everyone is expected to follow.

Experienced golfers know how important it is to make tee time at a prestigious course like Bethpage, so we were sprinting up to the tee box to avoid as much embarrassment as possible. We all ran up to see one of the most awkward moments of my life: Wild Bill standing in the center of the tee box blocking anyone from teeing off. He was literally backing old men away and not allowing them to skip our turn.

My brothers and I were immediately the least popular people on the course because of our association with our dad. To get out of trouble, our goal was to tee off and just get away from the clubhouse as quickly as possible. We figured that once we got on the course that we would get away from the crowds of people hollering at our father. Keep in mind, Wild Bill had no intention of actually golfing. In fact, this is a common theme in many Wild Bill stories: He doesn't actually participate in the activities that he arranges. He "simply" sets them up and stays in the background when possible.

After we tee off, he tried to tell the starter that he was our caddy and that he would be accompanying us throughout the round. I was surprised my father even knew what a caddy was, but at this point, I knew we were overstepping our bounds. My brothers have already left the tee box and I told him that we would be fine. His work was done.

Only he wasn't done. After teeing off, we walked very quickly down the first hole. As I mentioned earlier, we were trying to get away from the clubhouse and all the old men who were pissed at us. Just as I was getting away from the commotion and thought things were settling down, I hear Wild Bill yelling from back at the tee box, "You forgot your bagels and orange juice!" He literally was walking down the first fairway screaming at us to come back and get our food.

Again, Wild Bill knows nothing about golf, but he is as cheap as they come and he knows that the food at clubhouses is very expensive, so he wanted to make sure we had economical nourishment to get us through all 18 holes. I jog back toward the tee box to meet him and quiet him down when he hands me a bag with a dozen bagels and a carton of orange juice. No cups. No butter. No cream cheese. No knife. Just bagels and a carton of orange juice.

At this point, I tell my father, "Dad, you did a great job today. We really appreciate everything, but how about you go back to the house, relax, and we'll come by after we're done playing our round of golf. Get the barbeque ready and we can enjoy the day when we return."

It seemed like he agreed with that plan and left the course. After a few holes, things finally start to settle down. We had gotten away from the group of angry old men, it was a beautiful day, and Scott was finally calming down and enjoying himself. The funny thing about Scott is he's actually a lot like Wild Bill - has similar mannerisms, likes to get things done, and quite frankly can be pretty irritable like my dad. In fact, given they are so much alike, they drive each other nuts.

When Scott was 18 years old and finally sued the electric company that failed to repair the power line that he stepped on, my mother recalls Wild Bill and Scott brawling outside the courtroom because my dad was too cheap to get a hotel for them to get ready. They drove eight hours from New York and Wild Bill wanted to go right to the courtroom instead of trying to clean up first. Scott was livid. Billy, on the other hand, handles Wild Bill very well.

He keeps things light by imitating him and poking fun at Wild Bill while he is in the middle of his shenanigans. So Billy was having the time of his life at Bethpage.

As we were approaching the 8th hole, my brother Scott mentioned, "You know, with all the craziness in getting out here and daddy fighting with everyone at the clubhouse, it looks like the day has really worked out." We had found our groove and were enjoying the day without dad screaming at the local golfers or running down the first fairway with bagels and orange juice.

As Scott went into his back swing for his tee shot and we hear a voice come from out of the nearby trees, "You guys need some fucking golf balls?" We turn around to see my father walking out of the woods of Bethpage golf course with about ten golf balls. To make matters worse, he wasn't only finding lost balls in the woods. He was stealing them off the fairways!

So you better not have hit a drive near the woods that day because Wild Bill was stealing golf balls for his sons and you could have been one of his victims. At that moment, Scott dropped his club and announced that he was done. Billy was hysterically laughing. I was caught in the middle: mortified at my father's complete disregard for etiquette but laughing inside because of his bizarre behavior. Still, I'll trade some pissed off golfers for a lifetime of laughter about Wild Bill's antics. Sorry Bethpage golf course and all the golfers who were trying to enjoy a nice round of golf.

6 US OPEN – PART II

So again, I get the late night phone call. This time, it's the
Wednesday before the 2002 US Open:

> WB: I hear there is some US Open golf event at Bethpage
> tomorrow.
> Me: Yes, there is.
> WB: You want to go?
> Me: Pop, you don't just show up to the US Open and get a
> ticket to this golf event.
> WB: Yeah...What's your point?
> Me: It's a very corporate event and tickets are probably
> over a thousand bucks.
> WB: Get your ass out here in the morning and we'll go.

As the youngest of four kids, I feel it is my Caldwell duty to
play along with my father's eccentricities as my siblings have had
to put up with him for more years than me. I think the three of
them could write a book or two of their own filled with stories
from before I was born. The next morning I woke up early and

drove out to Bethpage. While approaching the golf course, I noticed that the exit to the parking lot was shut down and they were denying public access to the golf course beyond that point.

My dad's instructions from the night before were to meet him at his favorite restaurant: BK Sweeney's. I spent a few minutes sitting in the restaurant parking lot trying to figure out how we were even going to drive up to the golf course given the extra security around the event. Just as I was starting to wonder if he would ever show up I saw Wild Bill approaching the restaurant...on a bicycle. Now my dad is not a small man. As a matter of fact, he's downright hefty. And he was not riding a nice bike. It was one of those old Schwinn bicycles with a banana seat. The best part: He was wearing a shirt that said "US Open Security" across the front. Somehow he had finagled his way onto the US Open security team. And better yet, he had a T shirt and badge for me as well.

This is so ridiculous that I can't believe it happened, but since he only had one bike I had to jump on the pegs and ride on the back as he peddled on one of the bike paths back to the golf course. We had to turn a few heads: Five hundred pounds of

Caldwell riding together on a 25 year old bike. And on one of the nicest golf courses in the world. Still, I'm amazed how most people avoid confrontation, especially when the two guys on the bike are wearing official t-shirts for the event's security detail.

You would think that my father would use this ploy to get into the event and then enjoy the day watching some golf. Not a chance. Never satisfied, he proceeded to conduct actual security for the event. He was checking people's bags, rejecting a few items here and there, telling employees where to set up tents, etc. I was mortified. In fact, it got to the point where people were coming to him asking questions about policy and how the event should be run. I vividly recall one very well-known company in particular asking Wild Bill if they could set up a barbeque and tent in a certain area. He told them no. He then "found" them a better area for them to set up their operations.

Of course the company believed he was really hooking them up so Wild Bill basically became their main point of contact at the US Open. Whatever they needed, they asked Wild Bill. He had access to all their resources, food, etc. It was almost like he was a part of their company, in addition to conducting security for the event itself. I was standing next to him and employees walked up saying, "Hey Bill, where should we put this?" Wild Bill answered with such conviction that I started to believe he was really involved. It was bizarre because it didn't feel like he was misleading them. It felt like he truly believed they needed him. He got so caught up in the act that I think he really believed he was a part of the security detachment and a member of this particular company.

As grateful as I was that he got me into the event, I had to leave him. Not only did I want to watch the US Open, but I couldn't believe what he was doing. It's almost as if getting me into the event was too easy that he wanted more - so he hijacked the security operations. What else was he going to do? He didn't like golf, already got me into the Open, so he might as well help out with security. He couldn't sit back and enjoy the event. So I left my father to watch some of the most prolific golfers in the sport.

About halfway through the day, I see my dad driving his own golf cart. He pulled up and told me to jump in. We proceeded to pull up to the practice greens where we watched the big golfers get ready for their rounds. We saw Tiger Woods, Sergio Garcia, and a bunch of other golfers as they were preparing for their rounds later in the day. At one point, we were about five feet from Phil Mickelson. While he was warming up in front of us, Wild Bill turns to me and said, "Isn't this the guy who chokes in all the majors?" There was no way he didn't hear us from that distance. Sorry Phil. If it makes you feel any better, this was before you went on to win four majors. Maybe my father was your motivation!

After this exciting (and nerve racking) day, I went home and told the rest of my family. I announced to my brothers, sister, and brother-in-law, that Wild Bill had some operation at the US Open and that they should join him before the four day event was over. On the last day of the event, my sister Doreen and her husband Jim made a trip out there for themselves. By that Sunday, he was even in more control. Wild Bill basically was running the security for the US Open without anyone realizing that he was never even part of the security force to begin with. He even had our family in the clubhouse with the players after their rounds. He was driving his cart around, yelling at people, and somehow completely in his element. The golf didn't matter to him. What mattered was that he managed to bluff his way inside one of the most prestigious sporting events for several days in a row. I'm certain he enjoyed that more than any of the golf he watched.

Wild Bill in Kosovo!!!

Wild Bill winning hearts and minds with the Kosovo locals

Matthew Caldwell

Some more Kosovo Pictures

Wild Bill in Police Station in Kosovo and w/Tom Green

Police vests for the Iraqi Police

Wild Bill introducing me to President Bill Clinton

Wild Bill introducing my brother Scott to Pope John Paul II

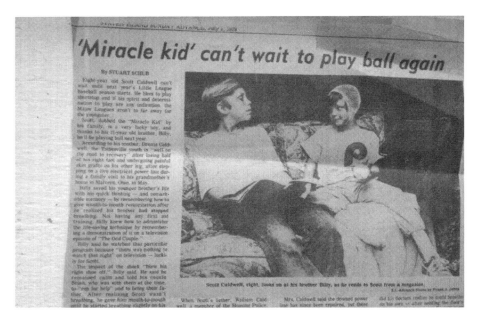

Brother Billy sitting with Scott during his recovery

General Barry McCaffrey administering my oath of office

Oath of office the family almost missed because of Wild Bill's tailgate!

Three generations of Caldwells enjoying a Yankee Game

7 FIRST DAY OF WORK

After I finished my military commitment from West Point and attended graduate school, I was fortunate to receive an offer at a prestigious firm on Wall Street. My father immediately starting busing my chops. Did an NYPD cop really raise a kid to go work at a white collar firm in New York City? Well, as you can imagine, he gave me a lot of flak for going to Wall Street, but of course deep down couldn't be more proud.

Before finishing school, I made a trip to New York to check out a few apartments and figure out where to live. I also wanted to drop by my new office to check in with the firm and say hello to a few people that I had interviewed with. Of course Wild Bill needed to be involved at some level. New York is his city and there was no way he was going to be satisfied just driving me around and letting me run such an operation alone. Despite being 30 years old, surviving West Point, having led soldiers in combat, and going to graduate school, my dad still didn't think I could do anything. He insisted that he drive me around to see a few apartments and help me navigate the city because I obviously could not do something like that without him along to guide me.

I finally gave in and allowed him to drive me around to see a few apartments, but I didn't want to bring him anywhere near my new building. The firm had just moved into a new building and the last thing I needed was my dad anywhere near my new employer. After driving around the city for a few hours, I intentionally had him drop me off a few blocks away from the office. I felt like a 12 year old kid having his parents drop him off away from school so none of his classmates would see him getting dropped off. I then said "Hey pop, I am going to head inside to talk to a few folks. I'll give you a call in a few hours and we can grab dinner. Sound good?" He said no problem and that he had stuff to do anyway. After all these years, I should have known better.

I walked in the building and met with various employees who I would soon be working with at the firm. In graduate school and college, students normally receive offers to work at firms well before they graduate. Because many firms will start a cohort of new employees all at once, it's common for their start dates to be at least a month or two after they finish school. In my case, it had been several months since I received my offer, so my goal that day was to reacquaint myself with the various people around the office. The meetings went well and it was a nice finish to a longer and uneventful day with my father.

After a few hours, I stepped outside the building, pulled my cell phone out, and began calling my father. As the phone started to ring, I looked up and saw another sight that I will never forget for the rest of my life. There was a private driveway in front of the office reserved for taxis and car services to pick up employees and clients of the firm. Well, Wild Bill, in his old green Buick, was parked dead center of the driveway. He was outside his car talking to a few taxi drivers. Oh yea, and for some inexplicable reason he's shirtless. Bare-chested. In fact, he had his driver's side door open and he was airing out his shirt over the top of the door.

The questions started to linger: How did he find the building? Why is he parked in the private driveway? Who is he talking to? Where is his shirt? Has anyone seen me? Do they know he is my father? Should I run?

In Wild Bill's defense, it was one of the hottest days on record in New York in May. To him, it made perfect sense to take off his shirt. The fact that he was standing immediately outside my future employer's building really wasn't a factor in his decision.

Realizing that I couldn't escape the situation, my plan shifted to getting him on the phone and telling him to drive down the street to pick me up. At this point, I didn't care if I took the Staten Island Ferry home. The last thing I need is someone from my new firm seeing me outside the building with my shirtless, hairy, and quite sweaty dad. I was only about twenty feet from him when I saw him reach into his pocket to get his phone out to answer the call. Before he answered, however, he made eye contact with me. This is where I ran into another one of my father's eccentricities: He is the cheapest man alive. He pulled the phone out of his pocket and starts waving it over his head while shouting, "I'm over here. I don't want to answer my phone and waste my minutes."

I couldn't believe it. In his mind, he didn't want to waste his crucial Verizon daytime minutes. I have to take a moment to step back and explain the absurdity of this situation. As you may know, Wall Street is a very professional workplace. Most employees wear suits and large banks are formal even for New York standards. Meanwhile, here is my father, essentially on my first day of work, standing outside the brand new headquarters building wearing fewer clothes than a homeless man chatting with all of the taxi and car service drivers. He was just one of the guys and of course screaming about his daytime cell phone minutes.

At that point, I just gave in. I walked over to my dad, gave him a hug and kiss, got in the car, and hoped nobody saw us. As we drove to dinner, my father looked at me and said, "What's the matter?" I responded, "Dad, why is your shirt off?" He looked at me in disbelief as if he couldn't understand what was wrong with me and said, "Because it's fucking hot!"

My girlfriend at the time, and someone I still admire to this day, Vanessa Torres, was literally on the back seat floor mortified because of Wild Bill's actions. She told me afterwards that he had her running all around the building looking for me. Vanessa kept telling him that I was fine, but he couldn't comprehend what was taking me so long. Despite the fact that I told him I would call when I was done. For people outside the family, Vanessa probably dealt with Wild Bill's shenanigans more than anyone else and this time was no different.

She could join the line of Caldwells that have their own books about Wild Bill when he tried to move her belongings one summer within New York City. I couldn't get off work as I was interning at a law firm so of course Wild Bill volunteered to assist. His notion of volunteering, however, meant that there was a new Sheriff in town. Vanessa watched as Wild Bill threw all her clothes and shoes in a box like the building was on fire. Shoes, dresses, photo albums, etc. All thrown around like dirty laundry. Vanessa called me in tears that he came in like a hurricane and everything was gone. He was then too cheap to rent a U-haul so he tied stuff to the top of his car and they both had to have their arms outside the window to ensure nothing fell off the car. After packing the car to the brim, he proceeded to drive 5 m.p.h down Lexington Avenue in Manhattan. Vanessa commented that everyone was beeping and cursing at him and he just drove down the street like nothing was wrong. As they drove south in Manhattan, I met them on the street to give them keys to the new place we were moving into. Wild Bill never came to a complete stop. He simply slowed down, I handed him the keys and he handed me a Diet Coke and kept driving. I stood there shocked. Vanessa told me later that he didn't want to leave anything behind in the fridge. She also learned that day that you can't question Wild Bill. You just have to take orders or take cover in the back seat.

Coming back to the current story, after hearing from my father about hot it was, I then kept quiet and listened to the sports radio talk that he normally has on in his car. There's really no sense in trying to teach an old dog new tricks. In retrospect, I came to realize that I was the fool. For better or worse, Wild Bill bows down to no one, and I have to respect that about him. As embarrassed as I was on my first day at my new job, I realized that I truly have the greatest father in the world. One who could care less about protocol - or anything else for that matter. He has taught me many life lessons, the first of which is "be yourself." If you do that, people will respect that more than anything else. The man will never change. However, now that I am integrated at the firm and have told this story countless times, he is now a legend and more popular than me. So I guess at the end of the day shirtless Wild Bill was the best introduction an employee could ask for.

8 WEST POINT GRADUATION

With thirty or so Caldwells swarming the West Point grounds,
I may have broken a record with the number of people who
attended my graduation ceremony. It was a wonderful day and my
family really enjoyed the festivities. One of the time-honored
traditions of West Point is that when a cadet graduates, he or she
chooses an active duty officer to recite their "oath of office" to
protect and defend the US constitution. Most cadets choose a
professor or mentor that had a strong influence on their young
careers. I was fortunate to have General Barry McCaffrey as a
professor at West Point. General McCaffrey was one of the most
decorated four star generals of his generation. Most of us were
intimidated to ask an officer of such high caliber to deliver the oath
of office, but in true Wild Bill fashion, I said "screw it." And true

to his reputation as being a soldier's general, General McCaffrey graciously accepted.

Given the antics of my family, I was very nervous about the encounter, so I tried to devise a simple plan to keep things from spiraling out of control. The graduation was set to end at around 11:30. I instructed all members of the Caldwell family to meet me at nearby Eisenhower Hall at noon after the graduation ceremony finished. General McCaffrey was having lunch there with several distinguished guests including the sitting President at the time, George W. Bush. The plan was for me to meet General McCaffrey at Eisenhower Hall, and he would step outside for a few minutes to administer the oath in front of my family.

My plan was fairly straightforward and easy to execute until Wild Bill took control. There was no way he was playing second fiddle when there were so many moving parts for him to tinker with. During the graduation, I heard him screaming from the stands that we should meet in Parking Lot A, not the original plan of Eisenhower Hall. As usual, he did this due to his complete disregard for the etiquette or formality of the ceremony. He kept yelling, "Matthew, meet at Parking Lot A. Don't go to Eisenhower

Hall." He did this without any recognition that there were another 800+ cadets graduating and their families were trying to watch the ceremony. Additionally, Parking Lot A and Eisenhower Hall were in completely opposite directions of the graduation ceremony.

I didn't have the slightest idea why he was changing the plan. I did know that I only had thirty minutes after the graduation to meet the General. I worried that I wouldn't have enough time to meet in Parking Lot A and then run to meet the general. And you never want to be late in the military. Wild Bill could care less. Parking Lot A was reserved for alumni who donate a large amount of money to the school. My father hasn't donated a dollar to West Point, but of course he had a spot in Parking Lot A. How? It's a question I find myself asking a lot in my life, but it's better not to ask questions with Wild Bill and just follow orders. It was great preparation for my time in the Army, but I wasn't really concerned about preparing for the Army right then and there. I mostly wanted to be on time for General McCaffrey.

Wild Bill probably found some cop or former security professional that was controlling the gate at parking lot A, gave him NYPD police hats and shirts, and worked out some sort of deal. My dad had a spot in parking lot A and he was going to use it whether we needed it or not. He didn't care who he kept waiting, including four star generals.

After the graduation, I ran up to meet my father. The problem, as I mentioned, is that the parking lot was on the opposite side of campus from Eisenhower Hall. I was ready to kill him before I even got there. When I arrived, my brother Scott had his suit jacket off and was sweating profusely. He was holding his two hands up in the air, telling me to stop, and screaming at me, "Just leave and go see the General. We'll all miss the oath. Just get out of here."

I came to the conclusion that my dad wanted to "tailgate" in his parking spot before heading over for the oath of office. He didn't care if that meant a four star general had to wait for him. He had the entire family corralled around his beaten up MPV minivan for this epic "tailgate." Being extremely cheap as always, the food and drink selection for this special tailgate was rather limited. In fact, all he provided was a dozen Dunkin' Donuts and a three liter bottle of Diet Cherry Pepsi. Again, there were 35 of us. Scott was yelling, "I am going to miss the most important day of my brother's life for a half of donut and swig of diet fucking cherry Pepsi." I couldn't believe what was happening, or really why, but I then followed my brother's orders and left to meet the General. I quickly changed from my cadet uniform into my new US Army uniform and ran to Eisenhower Hall.

When I arrived to greet the General, I explained to him that my family might be late. He was very patient and started asking questions about my family. "Now what is your mother's name?" "What is your girlfriend's name?" I explained and made small talk with him while hoping my family would make it there in time. Just when I was about to give up, we saw a herd of Caldwells running over the horizon. My mother with her bright red hair was leading the pack. She wasn't going to miss this day and the rest of the Caldwells followed suit.

Somehow they made it only a few minutes late. Of course my father showed up with NYPD shirts and a hat for the General. Most people were dressed in suits and dresses while he was wearing his usual informal gear with cigar ashes and coffee stains. My brother Scott more or less had a nervous breakdown back in parking lot A and was trying to regain his composure. I wish we could find the video of my brother pacing and trying to calm himself before meeting the General. I think Scott was more excited about the oath of office and meeting General McCaffrey than I was. But just like any other situation involving my father's antics, it all somehow worked out. General McCaffrey gave a great speech and my family had a wonderful time. Despite all the drama, we had a great story to tell. Sorry General McCaffrey for being late and dealing with a crazy family.

9 GROCERY SHOPPING

My father retiring from the NYPD made life very rough for the rest of us. He now has nothing to do. He sits around all day thinking and then we will receive a frantic phone call about selling stocks, looking up cheap flights, clipping coupons, and so on. One of the hobbies or tasks he has also picked up is grocery shopping. This goes back to his strong opinion that none of us can do anything, so he takes it as his obligation to shop for everyone in the family. We call it his personal paper route. Just as a teenager drops off newspapers in the local neighborhood, Wild Bill stops by all the siblings' homes (and my mother's!) and delivers groceries. It's a very nice gesture, but we have to sit and listen to his lectures on each product:

"I got this tomato sauce for 30% off."
"How much do you think these water bottles were?
"You need paper towels? Here's a 40 pack for half price."
"I got every salad dressing in the place. Whatever you need."
"Drink this, it was cheap."

It got to a point where he stopped by my brother Scott's house four days in a row talking about all the deals he brokered. My sister in law, Alicia, who does a great job handling Wild Bill, was like, "Bill, I just have no room for all this stuff. I love you and all, but you have to slow down here." Wild Bill hasn't stopped one bit. To this day, you walk in his house and he has a full dining table with all coupons he has clipped and a strategy of when he will be visiting the stores.

During his shopping escapades, Wild Bill found a local Pathmark supermarket that launched a marketing strategy where any customers that found an expired item on their shelves would receive a fresh version of the same item free of charge. This was a huge mistake. They obviously didn't account for a customer like Wild Bill. First, he memorized the expiration dates of all the products that he needed. Then, he would arrive at the store very early on the day of the expiration date, and pull off all the items before the employees had a chance to remove them from the shelves.

The store's staff couldn't understand how this strange man was finding so many expired products in their store. They quickly learned that they needed to remove the expired products a few days before the actual expiration date or else they would lose a bunch of money.

Of course, this did not stop Wild Bill. He then started hiding certain items behind others so the staff wouldn't know when they had expired. For example, he would place a carton of eggs behind the Captain Crunch cereal and then recover the eggs on the expiration date. He more or less created a scavenger hunt for the store staff if they wanted to keep up with him. Needless to say, Pathmark couldn't keep up with him and quietly ended the program ahead of schedule.

I have always said the worst thing that could have happened to the family, and the rest of the world for that matter, was Wild Bill retiring from the NYPD. He wants to be everywhere and doing something at all times. The NYPD did a good job of keeping that impulse in check, but retirement meant he needed a new outlet for his energy. Sorry Pathmark for interrupting your expired products marketing program.

Email to Neil Prakash:

Again, I thought it would be interesting to keep the email below in its purest form:

So I call my dad last week and ask what he would like for Father's Day. He gave his typical response: "Too much to do. Got no time." So I planned something with my sister to have a few people over her house. However, there was work to be done beforehand.

Wild Bill picks me up at 0800 on that Sunday. We head to "Jimmy's" for our free haircuts. Apparently, my father found this special blade for Jimmy's razors back in the 1970's when Jimmy first opened up shop in Brooklyn. It was a hit and Jimmy did really well. According to Jimmy, "Bill really put me on the map so I have owed him ever since." I guess three decades of free haircuts hasn't paid the bill quite yet. Then off to my father's dentist. My dad heard me talking to my brother one day about my student health insurance plan in graduate school. It does not include dental so I pay out of pocket for my cleanings. So of course we walk in around 1100 on Father's Day and after a few hats and NYPD t-shirts later, I walked out with a free cleaning and toothbrush.

We then head to "Hassan Shop" (the Caldwell mechanic). We pick up my brother Billy's car, which was mine when I was in college, but has been recycled throughout the family. Billy crashes about 2.5 cars per year so he's stuck with my 1997 Camry. Not allowed to get anything else. Billy's car had stalled on the highway and being that he is 42 years old, he tried to handle the problem himself. However, my father found out and went bananas. He got a trailer from "Hassan Shop" and picked up Billy's car at some Staten Island auto shop. In my dad's words "some Staten Island idiot tried to charge your brother 700 bucks to fix his damn car."

Now it's time for Costco. We have to go there because, as my father's puts it, "Nobody gives a shit about your mother and we need to do some shopping for her." Of course we all care deeply about mom, but this makes Wild Bill feel better that he's the poor soul who has always does the shopping. Believe me; he wouldn't let us do a thing for her because we "get ripped off at all the stores." We walk into Costco and the whole store knows him.

They give him the rundown on what's on sale. I have never seen anything like it. I was waiting for them to just bring him a cart full of his favorite food.

We get to my sisters by 3pm. He walks in, throws my nephew in the pool, tells him to learn how to swim, and tells the rest of the family how much he got done before arriving at the party. So I am now 29 years old, but still use my dad for haircuts, teeth cleanings, shopping, and auto repairs. This was the perfect Fathers Day for Wild Bill!

10 YANKEES

I was six years old when the Mets won the World Series in 1986. As is the case with most kids that age, I was very impressionable, so it was "cool" to be a Met fan. By the time I was about 8 years old, however, my father sat me down and said: "Son, if you want to be a Caldwell, you need to be a Yankee fan."

I remained unconvinced until a year later when the Yankees were in last place. I was watching one of the last games of the season against the Detroit Tigers who needed the win in order to capture the Pennant. The game didn't mean anything to the Yankees because their season was already lost. Well, in the 9th inning with the score tied, Steve Sax from the Yankees scored on a sacrifice fly ball to win the game. I will never forget Sax barreling into the catcher to score the final run and watching Yankee

Stadium go wild. My father jumped up and screamed, "You see, that is Yankee F'n pride! That is why you need to be a Yankee fan!" That day I was blessed and anointed as a Yankee fan.

I have a lot of great Yankee memories growing up. My father used his police connections to get many of my friends and family into the stadium to watch their games. Throughout my childhood, I was lucky to watch a large number of games from the House that Ruth Built.

There was one experience in particular that I will never forget. It was opening day in 2002, and a small number of West Point cadets were selected to carry the American flag on the field during the national anthem. As a well known die-hard Yankee fan at West Point, I was one of the cadets picked for the assignment.

When we arrived at the stadium, I had commented to one of my friends that I was surprised my father didn't want to get involved in the operation. I was telling my fellow cadets how I grew up going to many Yankee games and it was a big part of my childhood with my dad. As I was standing in the left field bullpen before game, I turned and spotted my father barreling around the stadium with a few cops. He found a few lieutenants that he knew from his time on the force and had them escort him around. At the time, I was holding a bat that one of the sergeants at West Point had given me in case I could get it signed by one of the players. Wild Bill got his hands on that bat and got Yogi Berra, Rudy Giuliani and a few other players and dignitaries to sign it for the Sergeant. His out of place access and braggadocio absolutely amazed all of the cadets. He was like a bulldog and the West Point officers in charge of us had no idea what to do with him.

As if getting into the stadium's bullpen and getting my baseball bat autographed wasn't enough, nothing topped his actions once we started carrying the flag on the field. There were about 25 cadets carrying a very large flag that we eventually unfurled once we were all out on the field. Well once I had walked on the field, I heard the words, "smile son!" I looked over my shoulder and there was my father standing on the warning track in left field. He had run out there to take a few pictures of his son walking on the field.

I recall the military officers that were supervising us yelling at him to get back in the bullpen. They weren't crazy about the fact that my dad was even hanging out with us in the bullpen to begin with, but as usual, he didn't care and ignored them while he did what he wanted to do.

For the rest of the game, we sat in the upper deck and the cadets with me really got a kick out of Wild Bill. He drove the officers crazy because he was the only person that didn't understand, respect, or answer to their authority. Of course, that only made the cadets in the group love him even more. At one point, he brought me down to seats closer to the field, which really fired up the officer because they were insistent that all of the cadets stayed in the same area. They obviously hadn't met Wild Bill before. There was no way we were sitting in the upper deck the whole time.

11 SAVING DREMA

For this story, it's important to explain a rather unique aspect of Wild Bill's life: He sort of has two wives. Although the situation is completely transparent, it is a pretty bizarre set up. He was married to my mother Drema for 23 years. They wound up separating, but never got a technical divorce. Since then, he still lives with his current "girlfriend" of another 25+ years. Now, my father fully supports both women. He spends a lot of personal time with his girlfriend, but spends most holidays, birthdays (even war zones), and other family gatherings with our family. I remember mentioning this situation to Vanessa when we first met and she said, "I guess I understand. I mean, who would really question Wild Bill anyway?"

In another interesting twist, my mother is actually closer with Wild Bill's family than Wild Bill is himself. Since my mother's side of the family lives in Ohio and West Virginia, she spends most holidays with Wild Bill's siblings, who are more local in the New York City area. This is probably more a credit to the character of Drema, but it's still interesting nonetheless. Additionally, my mother and father probably speak every day. This was not always the case as I am sure there was a lot of animosity when they initially separated, but there are few things that eventually brought them together.

First, my father was diagnosed with leukemia, which he is still battling today. I think this created a sense of perspective that was not present in the past. Second, having a son at West Point and then serving overseas created limited time for the family to get together so I think they were forced to see each other more often. Finally, and probably the most important factor, my mother suffered a terrible spinal infection, which has left her essentially paralyzed from the waist down to this very day. Given her condition, my father has taken on greater responsibility in accompanying her to the hospital, keeping the house in order, and also travelling with her to help her get around. And of course buying her groceries at a discount! So despite being separated, my mother and father have a very unique relationship. They continue to be cordial in honor of spending time with the family and my dad still does many things for my mother to help her with her condition. While it makes things easier for all of us, I won't deny that it is rather peculiar.

My mother's medical complication actually began when I was a senior at West Point in 2002. She had a stomach ulcer and went to the hospital for what she thought was a routine procedure. While cauterizing the ulcer, the doctor mistakenly cut her epiglottis in her throat. She proceeded to bleed internally and many doctors at this Staten Island hospital could not figure out where she was bleeding within. At this point, I don't think my family understood the ramifications of this accident. I remember my brother Scott calling me and saying, "Let me go to the hospital and see what the deal is. I am sure she is fine. If there is an emergency, are you able to leave West Point?" I informed him that I would need a phone call from a family member to request emergency leave.

After a few hours, I will never forget my brother calling with an exasperated voice: "Who do I need to call to get you out of West Point? You need to come home." I quickly realized that my mother was in danger. After speaking with my superiors and getting approval for emergency leave, I went home to visit my mother in the hospital. She had been on a respirator for a few days now (Caldwells sure like their respirators!!). She was losing blood by the day.

In the end, she wound up losing fifteen pints of blood when adults only have ten pints in their entire body. So my mother was left with transfused blood in her body. We continued to question the doctors on why they couldn't find the source of the bleeding, how we would finally to resolve this, and what next steps we should take. During these trying days, my dad was on a cruise with his girlfriend that I mentioned above. We opted not to contact him as we figured we could handle the situation ourselves. On day four, however, my mother was still on a respirator and the minor ulcer issue was quickly becoming a crisis. And in times of crisis, you call Wild Bill.

To this day, I still don't know how my father got off a cruise ship in the middle of the Atlantic Ocean and arrived at the Staten Island hospital. All I know is after we informed him of the situation; he was at the hospital a few hours later. I wouldn't be surprised if he ordered a damn helicopter to pick him up on the cruise out at sea!

What occurred next is another sight that I will never forget (there are a lot of them at this point): Wild Bill came storming around the corner of the hospital hallway like a freight train. My brothers and I felt a bit emasculated as we weren't able to figure out what was wrong with my mother and how we should proceed. Well it was time to move over because the real Captain was in control.

Within minutes, he had every doctor in the hospital working on my mother. My dad forced their hand to move my mother to the much more prestigious Mount Sinai hospital in Manhattan. The problem, however, is that in order to transfer my mother to Manhattan; she needed to go on a temporary respirator, which only worked for about forty-five minutes. On a Saturday night in New

York City, the doctors feared that they wouldn't be able to get my mother to Mount Sinai in less than forty-five minutes.

Wild Bill assured everyone not to worry. Given his NYPD connections, he ordered a police escort to accompany the ambulance transporting my mother to Manhattan. There were five cars driving in the escort – two police cars, two cars with Caldwells, and my mother's ambulance. I remember driving in one of the cars worried sick about my mother's health. I was counting the minutes to make sure we got to Mt. Sinai in time. I even had someone else drive the car as I was too stressed to concentrate on keeping up with the police escort. Definitely not one of my finest moments, but it was true I was trembling.

Throughout all of this, while my mother's life was in danger, Wild Bill was in his element – barking orders as if he was on the streets of Brooklyn. He was sitting in one of the cars in front of me with a cowboy hat on, smoking a cigar, and his foot outside the window. As much as this drove me crazy, it was a sense of relief. I recall screaming to everyone in the car, "What the hell is he doing? Why is he so relaxed and enjoying this?" Well Wild Bill loves crisis and I can tell you as a nervous son, it was delightful to witness.

Once getting to the Manhattan hospital, within hours the doctors found the source of bleeding and helped stop the internal bleeding. My mother eventually healed, although several years later she had an infection in her spinal cord that has left her in a wheelchair to this very day. Although these two traumatic events are not directly linked, many believe her history of poor blood flow throughout her body was a catalyst to this spinal infection. However, my mother continues to keep her optimistic spirit and is a true model of perseverance for the rest of our family. In addition to everything else she has done, it made me realize that she is the true backbone of this family. Wild Bill himself has even admitted that he wouldn't be able to deal with the tough obstacles thrown at my mother.

In life, I have learned that you want to see leaders in control and thriving under pressure. People need someone to rally around and look up to. I thought I would experience this in the military while serving in combat. In hindsight, however, I realized that I found it well before the military. I found it right at home with

Wild Bill.

CONCLUSION

I share these stories simply because people around the world need to know about this great man and all of the insane things he has done for his children. My point is not to encourage people to navigate to war zones or hide eggs in the cereal section at your local grocery store.

My message is that parents around the world should look themselves in the mirror and ask if they are putting forth their best efforts with their children. Maybe ask yourself, "What would Wild Bill do?" the next time you are contemplating going the extra mile for your kids.

Wild Bill is the type of father that I hope to be someday. I may not have the same courage as Wild Bill, but hopefully I can show the same love and affection that my father has showed for all

of his children. I also want to recognize again that all of this came

about because of our wonderful mother. Behind every great man is

a great woman, and there is no better example of that than Wild

Bill and my mother, Drema Caldwell. Despite separating when I

was 5 years old, they have maintained a cordial relationship after

23 years of marriage and still get along well today. They do this in

a purely selfless way to keep the Caldwell family intact. While

Wild Bill may provide all the entertainment and funny stories, it's

Drema who steered the ship and made us such a great family.

Mom, thank you again for putting up with this maniac for so many

years and keeping us all together.

One of the craziest aspects of this book is that these stories

were mostly during my lifetime. I am the youngest of four with

nearly ten years between me and my next oldest sibling, so you can

imagine how many other stories occurred before I was born.

Finally, Wild Bill set the standard on how to be the best father:

He would do anything for his kids. He may break a lot of rules and

annoy just about everyone around him, but he gets it done. I hope

this book serves as motivation for fathers everywhere to pick up their game! God Bless you Wild Bill. Thank you for all the memories. Thank you for enabling us to be good storytellers. I will never forget my 23rd birthday and everything else you have done for us.

AFTERWORD

It took me about two years to complete this book. While the stories are well known and needed little research, it still took longer than I expected. During the process, I grew an immense appreciation for authors as it takes a ton of time to put pen to paper, even for material you know so well. During that time, I only told a few people about the book, but nobody in my family. My goal was to keep it as a complete surprise. Plus, I am not sure anybody in the family could keep the secret anyway!

One of the motivating factors for finally completing the book was my father's surprise 70th birthday in April of 2013. I wanted to be able to provide my father a copy in time for the party. And while I accomplished this feat, Wild Bill's antics on that very day deserved another section in the book. So I wrote the following after the infamous presentation of the book.

Wild Bill is a very difficult person to surprise. He always has to be aware of what is going on, likes to plan, asks many questions, and doesn't allow anyone else to be in control. I knew if we were going to surprise my father, we needed to do something that was a part of his normal routine and hopefully he wouldn't catch on.

That's when we decided to turn to Atlantic City. My mother and father go to Atlantic City about twice per month. The two of them can sit in front of the slot machines for hours and have the best time of their lives. They have been going to the Trump Marina (now the Golden Nugget) for ages.

During my first few years working on Wall Street, I would organize a trip for a few of my friends to meet my parents at the Golden Nugget. My father was in his glory during these trips. I would show up with about seven friends from work and let my father run the show. He would gamble all day with my mother, which entitled him to a few free rooms. He would then turn those rooms over to my friends and leave for the night. Thus, all we had to do is show up and Wild Bill gave us free rooms. Nothing could make Wild Bill happier – we got free rooms and we "needed" his assistance to book us a hotel. As if a few guys in their 30's couldn't figure out booking rooms. We obliged because this is what makes Wild Bill tick.

So on April 6th 2013, one week prior to Wild Bill's actual 70th birthday, I asked my father to coordinate this operation once again. We did the usual: he arrived at my apartment in New York City, I took the groceries upstairs to my apartment (because none of us know how to shop), we then proceeded to pick up my mother in Staten Island, and then off to Atlantic City. I also brought along a buddy from work, Robert Burns, to cement the cover story that this was our annual Atlantic City trip. Rob got a live data point of how Wild Bill operated throughout the ride – he lectured Rob on his E-ZPass deals and provided me a ton of guidance on how to drive his car.

My plan was a very simple one. At the Golden Nugget, when you walk in the front door, there is an escalator and elevator that bring guests to the main reception area. The escalator and elevator leave guests about thirty feet from each other, but on the same floor. Given that my mother is in a wheelchair, my parents always use the elevator. So my plan was to take the elevator, as they do normally, and thirty-five Caldwells would be waiting where the elevator lets off. I also positioned my mother and friend Rob in front of Wild Bill so that he would be the last person on the elevator. That way when they got to the top, Wild Bill would be the first person to get off.

The plan was playing out beautifully until one unaccounted for occurrence: the elevator was taking too long. With my thirty two years of experience in operating with Wild Bill, I could feel the pit in my stomach as I knew Wild Bill wasn't going to wait for the elevator. I begrudgingly turned around and it was like a movie: Wild Bill was gone…storming up the escalator.

I immediately screamed at my father about having to take the elevator. In hindsight, it was clearly obvious I was overreacting because we wanted to do a surprise at the top of the elevator. He turned around and screamed at me, "Matthew, you take care of your mother. I need to get rooms for your buddies." My plan backfired. I got my father so excited about the "cover story," which was helping my fellow workers get rooms, that he was so enraged about accomplishing the mission and insistent about taking over the operation. Throughout all these years, I never learn.

I then ran up the escalator after Wild Bill. When he arrived at the top of the escalator, he ran towards the front desk as if the building was on fire and he was saving the world. Behind him, about thirty feet, my whole family stood by the top of the elevator exit. Luckily, my niece Cerina, noticed our antics and gathered the whole family to alert them that was Wild Bill was on the loose and no longer coming up the elevator. The family was behind Wild Bill as he stormed towards the reception area. I was yelling, "Dad, Dad, stop, stop!" He then turned to me and said, "What the fuck do you want?" With that, better than I could have scripted, the whole family screamed "Surprise!!!!"

My father stood in absolute shock. Surprise parties are so genuine in that if you really surprise someone, it's a true moment in one's life where the person doesn't know what to do. Wild Bill stood there for about ten long seconds. I can only imagine all the questions running through his head: Why are they here? Why don't I know about this? Who is paying for this? Is it is my birthday already? Where are Matt's friends?

I kept reiterating to my father, "Dad, it's your 70th birthday. We organized a surprise party for you. People celebrate birthdays. Dad, do you understand?" He really didn't know what to do. He couldn't believe he was so blindsided and the trick was on him all along. With that, he looked me straight in the eyes, didn't break a smile, and said, "Did you get your mother a fucking handicap room?" Even during his surprise 70th, he was worried about others.

At this point, we proceeded to a private room that my family reserved for the birthday party at the Golden Nugget. We had a great few hours reminiscing about my dad's shock and all of the Wild Bill stories. At one point, my brother Billy approached me about gathering the troops as he wanted to make a grand speech. He had been working on it for months and was ready to bring down the house. Just like he did for Scott's 40th.

Well Billy sure delivered. He basically touched upon everyone in the room telling a story about how they depended on Wild Bill and what crazy things my dad did for them. For himself, Billy commented, "I thought my name was Fuckko until the age of 5. My mother put Billy on my schoolbag and I was very confused.

Daddy always calls me Fuckko." Billy had everyone laughing hysterically. It was now Scott's turn. In true fashion, Scott delivered a very straightforward, heart-felt speech. Scott told the story of when he lost his foot (see Chapter 4). When he awoke from his coma, but still sedated, the doctor informed my family that they needed to remove Scott's foot. The family had to decide whether to do it now as he was sedated or to wake him up, so the family could prepare Scott for the operation. There was really no choice in the matter as we knew Wild Bill was going to deliver the news.

As Scott describes the story, it wasn't the most graceful speech. Wild Bill opened with, "Son, we need to remove your foot." After delivering the crushing thesis statement, Wild Bill then assured Scott that he would be just fine. "Scott, you are a Caldwell. We fight through everything and never let anything stop us. We will battle through this as a family and you will be back to normal in no time." Scott's rendition of the story is much better than I can relay here, but I can assure you there wasn't a dry eye in the room.

At this point, my family was going through a roller coaster of emotions. We went from the excitement of surprising Wild Bill, to the utter laughter of my brother Billy, to the very sentimental Scott reliving his tragic accident. I had a long speech prepared before I presented my dad with the book, but as I perused the crowd, I didn't know how much more my family could take. So I took the microphone, and with the crowd having no idea about what was going to happen, delivered the following short speech:

> Dad, you have obviously done a number of things for all us in this room. Billy has already recounted some of these epic stories while Scott touched on your leadership, especially in times of crisis. I know for me, I have told these stories all over the world. Whether it was Staten Island, West Point, US Army, Northwestern, Wall Street, or everywhere in between, the reaction is always along the lines of: "Wow, you need to do something with this material. I have never heard such unbelievable stories in my life." Well Pops, I did do something about it. In your honor, I wrote a book!

With that, my family sat in amazement. Never had it been so quiet in a Caldwell setting. I reached beneath a table, pulled out the book, and handed it to my father. He tried to laugh it off at first, but his eyes quickly filled up. Never have I seen Wild Bill shed a tear!

Matt chasing Wild Bill after he ran up the escalator

Matt trying to explain the surprise party to Wild Bill

35 Caldwells yelling surprise!!!

Mom coming out of elevator after we ran up the escalator

Scott in true sentimental form

Billy lighting the room as always

Parents laughing at Billy's speech

Family before the presentation of the book

Matt presenting book to Wild Bill

Wild Bill trying to hold back tears

Matt and Wild Bill after presentation

Wild Bill giving speech after book presentation

Wild Bill and grandson James

The Caldwell Family

After the party, the Caldwells were enjoying Atlantic City. Wild Bill was nowhere to be found. I searched his room and he was reading his own book!

Matthew Caldwell

ABOUT THE AUTHOR

Matthew Caldwell grew up on Staten Island, NY, where he went St. Joseph by the Sea High School. He then attended West Point military academy from 1998-2002. Upon graduation, he spent five years in the U.S. Army, where he conducted a combat deployment to Iraq, peacekeeping operations in Kosovo and spent the rest of his military career in Germany preparing soldiers as they deployed to Iraq and Afghanistan. After completing his military commitment, he received a joint JD/MBA degree from Northwestern Law School and the Kellogg School of Management. He currently works in finance in New York.

23421977R00073

Made in the USA
Lexington, KY
10 June 2013